That Mulberry Wine

Wesleyan New Poets

That Mulberry Wine

Janet Sylvester

Wesleyan University Press
Middletown, Connecticut

Some of the poems in this book appeared originally in these journals: *The Agni Review*: "Managing the Composition"; *The Bennington Review*: "Conneaut Lake"; *Cimarron Review*: "Horseshoes"; *Ontario Review*: "Cambridge, 1981," "Hard Strain in a Delicate Place"; *Prairie Schooner*: "Mrs. Gardner's Picture"; *Seneca Review*: "That Mulberry Wine" (as "My Grandmother Marries My Grandfather"), "The Woman in the Wall"; *Tendril*: "Arrowhead Christian Center and No-Smoking Luncheonette," "Interval," "Solo." "The Late Show" first appeared in *The Morrow Anthology of Younger American Poets*.

This book is supported by a grant from the National Endowment for the Arts.

All inquiries and permission requests should be addressed to the Publisher, Wesleyan University Press, 110 Mt. Vernon Street, Middletown, Connecticut 06457.

Distributed by Harper & Row Publishers, Keystone Industrial Park, Scranton, Pennsylvania 18512.

LIBRARY OF CONGRESS CATALOGING IN PUBLICATION DATA
Sylvester, Janet, 1950–
   That mulberry wine.
   (Wesleyan new poets)
   I. Title.
PS3569.Y46T48   1985   811'.54   84-22053
ISBN 0-8195-2126-4 (alk. paper)
ISBN 0-8195-1127-7 (pbk. : alk. paper)

Manufactured in the United States of America

First Edition

Wesleyan New Poets

For Mary, John, Nellie, Stephan, Louisa, El, and my teachers, Dave, Ellen, and Louise.

Nothing is ever the same as they said it was. It's what I've never seen before that I recognize.

—DIANE ARBUS

Contents

1 The Whiteness of the Child

Return

Swallowing the green fruit of gutturals,
the ersatz bread of vowels, a bitter breakfast,
we practice the foreign song. Expended breath,
it sways like a chimney above our heads.
When the long car glides into the schoolyard,
it is the afterimage against my eyelids
when the sun is bright. Animal-quiet,
we file into the thicket and hide.
Among burdock and cornflowers, my cat
finds me, his instincts more refined
than the soldiers' eyes, which require
a burning building to flush us.
Such blackness. Children in red dresses
genuflect before it and I stand still in line,
my heart a bucket plummeting from the well's rim.
As if hunger weren't enough.
I know nothing of pity, but that his face is pitiless,
and his hands.
The cat's body settles beside mine and we rise
a moment, above our clothes.
Around us, sunlight swivels
into position. My head, pure sense of direction,
presses into it.

This is a dream, you understand.
An animal that prowls, invisible in a field,
its hide transporting seeds,
its cries nudging my sleep,
as babies twist before we see them
in the birth rind. In which life
did I smooth my dress on the bedspread
after school and look down the ribbons of my slip
past spread knees into the hand mirror
given me by my grandmother, and touch my body

as if it were the first to be inhabited,
outside, heat simmering in the garden
and the folk song I didn't know beginning
at the back of my throat, death
again revocable, beyond their logic.

Conneaut Lake

Hunched in my red jacket,
I sat with the retarded girl at dock's end,
dangling legs and trying a cast, occasionally,
with my bamboo pole. We didn't talk,
unless it was her wordless gesture, lifting out
her string, at its end a safety pin
for me to put a worm to. I prayed for anything,
even the smallest sunfish, to run against her hook.
Last night there, I told her about Old Baldie,
the muskelunge whose cave
was twenty yards from where we sat
over pinkening water.
Teeth that could take your leg off,
a body scarred white by his escapes—
I wanted to see in her eyes the terror
I felt, the shiver of conspiracy to weld us.
Now, she mumbled, tongue thick against her lower lip
as the biggest fish I had ever seen leaped
where I pointed, almost suspended in its arc
above the boardwalk on the opposite shore.
A woman came to take her in then, but I stayed,
waiting for the fish to show again
as bats swung from the willows that hid our cottage.
Now, I commanded over and over again,
but nothing happened. *Now*, I say it now,
wondering at her, as I wait for checks to come,
for someone whose touch will last. All night,
I tried to warm the damp sheets of my bed,
saying, *Now. Now.* Near dawn,
something huge splashed not far from shore.
I ran through the shadowy house, down
where grasses chilled my ankles,
but the lake was grey, calm.
It might have been the only word she knew.

That Mulberry Wine

Cross-legged in my pinafore,
I picked at lacy socks and twisted a curl
around and around my finger.
Such perfect boredom, sitting at her feet
Sunday mornings, the bedroom stuffy
as she lipsticked and powdered herself,
sweat trickling into her corset. She got up,
let fall a dress over arms stretched above her head.
From the drawer, fragrant with handkerchiefs,
I chose a ring to try on. I wear it now,
the marcasites here and there missing,
its amethyst scratched.
Why she ever told me then about her beau—
arriving with his derby and borrowed car
for their picnic at the lake: she ninety-eight pounds,
hair straight-braided to her hips, and he,
a printer just in from Kansas,
finding an excuse to take off coat, string tie,
and shirt so she could see him, broad-chested,
if a little pale, throw down apples from the tree—
I don't know; I was only eleven—
my white dress reflected in the vanity
as she talked. Mouth gone dry, I heard them
smooth the blanket down
in among orchis and wintergreen. She arranged
two thimblesful of mulberry wine
and chicken her mother had fixed.
I was hungry. *Wait now*, she said,
as I balanced on one leg and he stood over her,
then swooped, awkward, to take a kiss.
Just you wait, she chided as he pushed her down.
I twist the purple stone back and forth on my finger
as she reached a hand with that new ring
and tore a stalk of brownweed out of the dirt.

Across his back, welts rose,
latitudes that haul me crazy to replicate
that day: the tree shaken, and under it
ground rooted with our new name.

Solo

The wrecked hedges could not quite close
behind me. A strip of road still glimmered,
the curb that had both stopped
and thrown me forward onto the lawn,
my blue bike above me, like a cage.

Abrasions, the doctor would say,
but I knew better. Passing through the green
trap cultivated for the neighbors' privacy,
I felt thorns scrawl their illegible messages
all over my uncovered skin.

I learned to read, letting words scrape by,
the velocity I knew then as me
full speed. Alone, I was overcome
by what I meant, but somehow safe.
I waited to love

and watched my neighbor, the long-shanked boy,
take care of hedges. I admired his expertise
at turning something green compact as concrete.
Behind my curtains, I watched his back in the sun.
He was clipping toward that place I had been through.

Arrowhead Christian Center
and No-Smoking Luncheonette

Each Saturday, our father downtown to work,
Eloise tagged along to watch me look
through flaked-gold letters at Arthur Benson, the Baptist.
While I dressed in a magenta sweater
and navy-blue felt skirt with a white poodle
pasted on it, she would roll her eyes
and make gagging noises at my choice of clothes.
This Saturday, Arthur wore chino pants
and white bucks and a pullover with no shirt underneath.
First, I lit one of my mother's Old Golds.
Arthur never looked up from his pamphlet.
Then I leaned on the revolving door,
hoping Eloise would go home, where I sent her.
The luncheonette smelled of cooking coffee.
Arthur, I said, positioning my chest against the counter,
*give me whatever I sign to prove I testify with you
to Jesus.* Arthur sauntered over to me
with a sheet of yellow paper that said:
I, blank blank, room for my name, *do renounce fornication,
smoking, dancing, and so on. I will take on the Lord.*
I signed. He asked me out. I had heard that about Arthur.
Oh, Arthur, you're so crazy, I sighed
as we warmed up his white Chevrolet.
Later, when all the windows were steamy, he kissed me
without opening his lips, and showed my hand
how far it could go inside his pants.
Arthur stretched his arms across the seat back
as I bent, hair falling around my mouth and what it did,
my head wedged against the steering wheel.
Black-haired bitch, he whispered, *your hair's like wire.*
I had never chugged anything till then
but knew how much, sometimes, you have to swallow in life
to prove a point.

Halfway down the street,
I could see my father waiting on the porch.
Eloise had spied on me and then gone home
to tell about that paper.
When he finished hitting me,
Daddy pulled me out into the yard under his fruit trees.
It was only February, but already
there were crocuses uncurling in the flower beds.
When he put his arm around me,
all I could think about was Arthur,
how he bucked and crushed my head over and over again
onto his body.
Daddy wasn't saying much, so I identified a constellation
that sinks down in the spring, Orion,
and wondered how much loafers stretch
from standing in muddy grass, and saw the moon
go in and out my father's breath.
I wedged my head then into that little cradle
below his shoulder, pretending,
I would never go near the luncheonette again.

Horseshoes

Maybe this.
Sun collapsed behind the Wonder Bread plant
pinks the stucco walls of this run-down house
where we gather.
The wind, my father tells me,
makes the angle.
Has loosened the blackened tree in the back lot
and scattered mulberries where we stand.
I know the angle is everything.
Left hand on my shoulder,
his right beneath my elbow,
he moves close in to coach my throw.
I have never played this game before
and pitch the rusty weight, hoping
the horseshoe, somehow, will fall in close.

Called from milking Nanny,
he stood up from a squat,
brushed at his white trousers,
patted the goat and turned:
Johnny Beans, go pick up Pop.
Seventeen, he went to fetch his father, drunk,
from among the family stumblers.
Nicola Maria. Grandfather.
   Nyeh Nyeh.
   Your father's a dame
   A wop's a dame
   because of his name.
Together they tangoed home,
performed their weekly wine-duet.
The boy, local football star, ran to win,
caught stylish, pose almost Egyptian,
twisted at the waist to face the camera,
his hands delicate, fingers barely splayed.

But that was later.
They are still in 1937,
all the unremitting grudges of the world:
an old man, hair grey brush fire,
who pukes the loss of his donkey cart,
1915, Foggia, and the drought,
and his son, who much too soon will crouch
explaining to team doctors
where between the legs he has been kicked.

Hefting their old horseshoe,
I sight down a grassless strip of yard
to a spike.
I have never played this game before.
Turning for luck,
I face my uncles lined up in their lawn chairs.
They will see whose child I am.
I reach, ignoring everyone leaning forward,
and rise, still not at the highest point,
that pitch when I can see my hand,
stained with dust and mulberry blood, release.
As if I didn't know this should happen.

Deep Summer Grass

I asked for honey and waited, hands in my lap
at the table, the stacked toast growing cold,
as my grandfather stood beside the stove
with its blue-enameled ship above the burners,
to warm a jar of sugar crystallized.
He raised it, toweled,
before the window where the cap unscrewed
and honey poured into the floor fan, spun
across the room, connecting Eve, hand-painted
on a plate, and relatives propped smiling
in their frames. Yellowjackets bumped
and conferred as they worked the screens.
The old woman and man laughed that day
petunias released their skirts
in the warmth of window boxes.

* * *

The day her body softly fell
into the lead vault, my grandfather and I
turned on the news,
and wrapped in the knobby afghans she had made,
slept, rocking a little. The dream in me
brushed her cheek with my lips
then reeled from its heat
to watch her chest not flutter again, breathing.
He said he had seen her favorite flower,
frilled and pink as her last dress.
Sitting beside the river today, I drowse
in sun that wakened us then at dawn,
the test pattern's static becoming a choir.
Death had swept and scrubbed the house,
and we were in it, making coffee,
not in the cemetery up the street,
where one bee, having emptied a gladiolus,
flew between white houses, each with its wife,

and found our open window. It wouldn't die.
Beside the honey, it drilled, curling into its fur,
its golden stripes what I saw
as it delivered in my palm the quick,
excruciating sting it was born for.

Wake

Hands locked around the bedpost, my grandmother
exhaled against the thrust
of a foot on her derrière
as her best friend, still alive in loose clothes,
strained the laces of a whalebone corset
to concord, a hard knot below the ribs.
The organdy dress and its waves of ruffles
settled above her head
as sweat changed lavender talcum
to paste, working its itch
on the hourglass figure wedding demanded.
Ramrod, she danced, wallow and grace,
like forty-five tons of humpback female
beside our boat today, lifting her fins
to motion in a slow roll, over and over,
the black flukes of her tail raised,
then slapping water with playful weight
enough to ruin our lives. I cannot forget
that white breast held to glisten
in the light, or the singing whistle
as she drew us in, calves
butting her side for the rush of milk,
watched from the reef
where calamity glides with its hammerhead
against her net, that impenetrable eye
the tide looks into.

2 An Excuse for Being

Hard Strain in a Delicate Place

That day, someone died down the beach,
both legs bitten clean at the knee.
No warning fin separated the wave
that pulled his limbs away.
Later, news would reconstruct the shark,
famous for its blunt approach and execution,
for its hiding game.
And the natives said what they do:
how terrible, but the price you pay
in tropical waters.

That must have been the meaning
of the siren wail that we ignored,
intent on your bad knee, its articulation
as we walked. Something swam into the joint
and stayed there, cracked and snapped
so only you could hear. *She sang,*
you sang, and spread your arms,
then winced above the pain. I caught you
off balance in a picture.

We imagined the whole world
was in order, if we could say it then
in someone else's words to the surf.
You stopped mid-stanza. *It hurts,*
it hurts. I should see a doctor.
The afternoon gave way as we walked
to the nearest dune and settled, silent,
the tick of my cigarette, newly lit,
audible only to me.
The sky looked faultless, empty.

During This Exposure

Someone bumps a flight, someone dies.
I adjust my seat belt, and check the airtight window
streaked with humidity, a memory of altitude.

"Crazy" curled from the transistor propped
beside me on the truck seat as I drove
what I couldn't do without down U.S. 95.
Camera ready, I waited to snap the regional freaks
we all become when too much alone.
The accelerator fit my naked foot
until it ached with momentum,
the heart's old settlements left behind.
Where were those hard-bitten women with teased hair,
country hits hidden in a trailer dresser?
I wanted to find a nightgown overlooked by maids
at Best Western, and let it spill through my hands,
like the time I convinced a lover I was in it
for the short run. With tourists
at a barbecue, I laughed, not yet immune
to gnats that haloed each of us and stung
what we couldn't cover, leading the majority
to relieve themselves with distance, and the Florida shore.
A housewife brought sweet tea
and her husband, pumping gas, whistled
Patsy Kline between his teeth
as cars, one by one, overtook the dark
of scrub-pine forests and concrete homesteads
looking embarrassed behind their palms.
I sat all night there, empty rockers moving
to the cicadas' creak
and no one appeared indispensable
as those faces, every feature jacklit
at a round table to say good-bye,
who touched me, staring

as though he had himself undone
the accidental button, cracked the joke
that opened me, night-blooming in South Carolina,
and no one I knew to tell.

The pictures were returned with stickers:
"out of focus," "movement during this exposure
(on part of camera or subject),"
"distance not correct." So much information
untranslated: those pink knots, hibiscus,
that blur, my house, and nothing done yet
for comfort, unpacked boxes a bulkhead
against the nightly dream of a red bird
that put its beak to my lips with a message
then disappeared so suddenly, mornings
it was unbearable to awaken.
I leaned on the drugstore counter
and knew that I would leave, carrying what I could
this trip—a drink, a book—
as in our walks beside the pond
when we spun another version of who did what
to whom, but no one mad for long,
ex post facto. I might have stayed,
missing autumn rain's drift across the meadow
and the thunk as eggplant fall, their sinews cut
before frost. Nearly home,
I admire stamina, dancing with itself.
I sip a Bloody Mary from the airline's plastic glass
and discard my opening line. Whatever happens,
I trust the flight plan back to another life
and, *sweet jesus,* I arrive.

The Red Suitcase

It stalls in the snow
beside the black bundles.
Her nightgown with its virginal, laced bib,
stockings wrapped in silver tissue,
manicure scissors in a kid pouch:
things folded or rigid, separate,
have begun to jumble,
and the girl with her frivolous hair
tucked into a cap for travel
feels the displacement of what she planned,
though she cannot see it. The wind picks up
her scarf and binds it
across her eyes, lashes thickening with ice.
Even in summer, the Sienese bell tower
would be unfamiliar as her own city
reentered by train.
Panic fumes through her, too stubborn
to kick or drag her life one more step.
She imagines her friend
stepping from his bed,
a book dropped next to the cup of wine
on the rug, as he moves to the window.
The natives slide by effortlessly
on skis.

Legacies

Esther Williams, every hair in place,
breaststroked underwater across the screen,
and smiling, broke into sunlight.
No one could touch her,
for all the world, like my mother,
breath withheld, her slender biceps
knifing the monumental blue of the pool.
Removing the fresh hibiscus flower
behind her ear, she threw it to the leading man,
and we turned to the blue-sheeted bed; the TV,
horizontal hold worn out, like a klieg light,
played across our faces.

That night wasn't mine.
Next to your blackout, I drowned
into this skin which is nothing
like the white and blue-veined masterpiece
we were directed to imagine.
I knew it would come to this:
the kiss spontaneous as a slap,
the nighttime good-bye, though no one warned me
you were just another man in white trunks
from the suburbs.

This is Esther Williams Week, a festival,
my mother said, reflecting on that swimming pool
thirty years ago. Mostly,
I watched ice widen into grease in her gin,
and how, squinting, she shifted in her swimsuit
to use the sun. Nothing could interrupt
what she said about old movies and perfect love.
Painted, her nails tapped against her glass,
like a code.

Gulf of Maine

Trees are a pretext, inexact,
as wind revolves in their leaves
turning the dark outside to surf,
something we are not sure of.
The ocean that night was warm,
the lighthouse tantalizing to couples,
blind then blinded, kissing in cars.
Tavern closed, he led me
over rocks to the family cottage.
The dark entry rapped me with its smell
of must and old linoleum, mildew
in the wood panels
covering half the walls.
I recognized each place
beside a lake where, a child,
I froze at spiders in the eaves,
tossed in the chilly sheets,
not knowing you reach an age
when nothing is out of character—
each act a vote cast by a new constituent
whose hand you cannot escape.
The waves, nearly but not quite, effaced
the palm-sized beach glass, opaque green,
I retrieved by flashlight
but hadn't planned to take when
I slipped away in the morning.

Retablo

What animates this blue is distance,
an inch of nerves behind the eye
that registers the world upside down
then corrects it, bang, quicker
than spit swapped in a kiss.
We want that friction, the evening
a blue body pressed against us,
and we rub its unexampled branches
with our thinking, the physical wish
to maintain half-light
with its ambitious lures.

I love it like love, the misconception
we have of one another, walking before dinner,
elbows so tightly locked,
we cannot remember sitting down
to polish shoes for a future
we don't want. A liaison,
its public secrecy, hidden positions
between us, the scrim
of appetite and denial,
with its coded excitement.

Eight of us sit in ourselves at table,
and no one moves with matches to the candles.
The blind hold out their hands as we do,
as if each movement they will make
were recorded and stored there.
No one touches. The future
circulates in us its pure seduction,
a form of charity
that precedes the first innuendo.

Interval

How do we feel? You asked that
in New Hampshire, birch leaves mottling silver
across our plates. I had no answer
as sheets, drying on a neighbor's rooftop
in New York, flapped and twisted
in a place I could have been.
It was so easy to lie beside you in the field,
my red shirt a pillow for your head.
The long shadows I love alluded to nothing,
the fraction of an hour we slept
in the same lit web, surrounded by flowers
insouciant as women who awaken drunk
with their own scent, and never dress.

Once, my mother pulled me on a sled
as snow billowed like linen from the pines.
A dog rushed past us in the dark
and snapped at the hand I waved to him,
stealing my glove. What threatened entered me then
so neatly, even the witness missed it.
It tracks me still, asleep,
where deftly you unbutton what I wear,
only to find me beside myself, but attentive,
fumbling to be present.

My mother's hair tumbled like wire around what hurt:
comfort, lethal simplicity.
How could we feel?
Here is the heart, I offered; it lives anyplace.
Cardinal, it winters in its own red feathers,
and stands the cold.
We might have slept all summer, blindfolded together,
and never answered, catching clothes as we ran
across the grass, half cut and stung to silence
in that public light.

Cambridge, 1981

The Salvation Army band disrupts the Square again.
Another Christmas toot starts the bars,
where the likes of you and me hush above a Scotch.
The French horn's image glitters in the window,
its carol faint as dust streaks on the 17th-century
paintings in the Fogg today. Two are called
"Portrait of a Man," "Portrait of a Woman,"
by Franz Hals, a master taxidermist,
who razored the facial plane just so at their cheekbones,
rubbed pink by Dutch humidity.
With a hand that curves like steel from its cuff,
each one clutches a glove, as if not to crush it.
Its watered silk runs cool against their palms
and draws the light. I would like to say
Hals does not erase their love—
the wife bent with a beer mug before the fire,
where her husband dandled the baby in its red sweater—
but that's interpolation.
To think they paid for it:
his usual dark dress ended the imposture,
and her shined ring suggested he was a cuckold.
They must have stood surprised together
for a moment. We drink and smile
as interruption stumbles, singing, into the bar.
Critics call him unassimilated life, the X
in orange stocking cap and scarf, disordering composition.
He orders a Coke. Now that he is at home
in the wavy stain above the bar,
I'll tell you how, in the present tense,
I crave the relaxation of their laws.
When Hals' mistress cried in a blue windmill,
salt scored the back of her hands, like a fugue.

The Woman in the Wall

She knots her fists in the curtains
and presses her face to glass
against who hears her. Cracked for air,
the window admits her expletives,
black ink that camouflages the woman
behind the words where I sit,
convinced that loneliness corrupts.
I know the sandbank where she gave up,
and god, with his artificial air, arrived
on vacation from the world's troubles.
She struggles, and four stories turn to one another
over their plates, the table set for duration.
No one wants her to cry. No one interrupts.
We recognize the odd fish that turns up
and how usual in the world pain is,
which never changes, but moves
from one room to another. I see her,
legs drawn to her chest
in her grey gown, as we have dinner
and wonder what god did there on the reef,
what hunger impelled him to beach
what he never planned to consume.
Nights, the rhythm of her life
drums us deaf to this edge
where we side-step, our faces turned
from her singular commitment.

Mrs. Gardner's Picture

I am not frivolous.
Havisham's wedding rags capped my decision
never to queen it, hands flat on knees,
my life, rotten cake on the table.
Balanced as high as I am in its branches,
today, I'll take tea in the mimosa.
Floating on picnic cloths,
my guests will drift and bob across the lawn.
I will climb down after a while
and then be attentive to each of them.
C'est mon plaisir, my personal motto.
Who sees up my skirts here
cannot guess the rehearsal of taffeta,
the decorous pleats that cover my knees.
Discretion does constitute part of my valor,
my privacy, as once
the large gesture amused me.
The portrait is also my pleasure.
Walking my lion across Boston Common, 1879,
I happened on John Singer Sargent, so shocked,
his palette fell on the path upside down.
Nine years later, he finished my painting;
we were never the same again.
In it, I turned full forward,
pearl ropes like snowberries
draped at my waist.
For him, I posed in black satin.
For him, my hands hung relaxed as though Jackie,
my dead boy, never dragged at them,
or I had not raised one, shaking a little,
to place it on the body of a man.
I wanted to love Sargent forever, but I am lonely.
I think my mind is all right.
I live on it.

The Monopolists' Revenue

In Swampscott, gardeners raze the lawns
within an inch of swimming pools,
austere in August. Behind bonsai
to the bought horizon, Puritan Road bends
like an acolyte above its Wall Street rags,
as strangers, their passes forged,
reclaim the beach, stinking
of jellies ruptured in a bank of seaweed.
Drowsy, a woman presses the stem of her wineglass
with red nails, their polish not yet dry
after a party where an EST devotee
proved what bore's one is the key.
With her rubber raft, she steps carefully
down the beachhouse shelf across grass
to our common plage.
This place smells like hell,
she says almost to me, as she settles
her knifelike shadow next to mine.
Two teenagers chase one another's tans
endlessly across the rocks. Burning together,
we anticipate their double grief,
while across the water, taut wings fold.
In the calm, we raise our Italian shades
and blink at one another, such priceless figures,
and at some scruffy dog, belly wet,
planting his paws like colonists
as he yaps at the waves.

Quarry

The mind unthreads.
Our faces waver, bodies move in sync
across its surface, the patch
unraveling where we stand,
faces pink in the wind.
This is sadness: the day
should not have heard what we said,
as in, *what's next*, the pattern
we are drawn to.
I recall your face
in a real blizzard and me too cold
for perseveration. Within treason,
you were all I needed,
your unmended nets the eye I slipped through
truly into dark. And you,
what an old joke, even you
seem crazy in this place
we once moved with our bodies.
I can't know what we will be.
Didn't we wear black at the beginning
when what we were added to the magic?
The whipstitch loosens.
Evening buys my cheap designs
as if we didn't strip once, cold, in a room
and begin the division: whatever we wanted,
from our strength, what we've become.

3 So Fast an Idea

1816: Mary Ann Woodhouse marries Gideon Mantell

1 The Fossil Hunter's Wife

Which is the shadow? The gosling or its imprint?
If it leaned toward language
would the little goose complain, saying,
Why have you given me your image,
a rush for cover so deep I see nothing
but safety just out of reach?
The wife of Gideon Mantell,
who lifted her starched petticoats in 1822,
overturned the rock
in which the first great lizard had lain
transfixed; held fast by its muteness
over time, she never entered her dark parlor
for fear the ferns would suffocate her,
the carpet turn to mud ankle-deep.
Bent over her, her husband
watched her face reflected in a teacup,
its features underpinned by carbon and minerals
sieved through fallen bodies into her form
destined to break, like them, in death.
The natural historian, surprised by love,
touched her face as she wept a little
for single cells percolating in her lungs,
in her throat, the slither of fish,
and behind her eyes, the lower primates
gesturing in a wild, comic way to the outside.

At night, she climbed a repeated staircase,
Freud's coital architecture
aligned with the ocean below, above it columns,
their capitals eerie in moonlight,

to turn in time and glimpse the face of the pursuer
whom she was sure she followed.
Once, she awakened in your room,
and stepped through her clothes to you
in the lit kitchen.
Imagine her solitude,
the floor strange to her feet as she approached.
Who knows what prior lives prepared you,
or the water you offered,
cold and ordinary, in its cup?
The membrane was so thin then, her hand
pressed through it to you
as the first blizzard let loose
flakes that penetrated the window frame
to star the distance between you.
You led her to the remade bed
as if you were friends, beautiful reptiles,
startled into their marsh by weather,
a bright rag of snowlight binding them,
as they labored to escape
what can never be done.

2   *Lewes, 1828*

At Castle Place, ammonite volutes
top our pilasters, like narcissi
on disciplined stems. The children have ridden
in rain for an outing
while I, Dear Girl of cramps, spasmodic asthma,
thumb *Frankenstein* and, propped on damp pillows,
hold fast the tilt of red debris they call mind.
Downstairs, Mantell and Cuvier
bend above our blazoned table, slaying afternoon
at cards. My heart turns the dumb queen
I was years ago at the box hedge,
four moons of Jupiter apparent in the glass,
the future a path lamplit from our entry window.
Now the ground releases more than trees
in the orchard, and I slide, each thought an intrusion
like fermenting fruit my husband leaves to ruin
as he tracks with pick and spade the shape
he conjured, his palm filled with teeth.
Gideon's offspring will be plaster, wire
joining blank eyes to the dark. In my dreams,
my white feet useless in the stirrups, I ride
as it pursues my mare to the hilltop
turning slurry under her hooves, and these hands,
all wrong direction where the bit wounds.

I wake to order: tea in a silver pot,
flawless bread on porcelain.
Once, we put an angel in the garden
and today, I watched its marble arm crack
into shadow where he moved it for a dig.
Even the bedposts rearrange, waver
in familiar firelight. As I turn these pages,

Shelley's face balloons, rising out of sight.
I do not care for skylarks,
or the sickening riddles of his wife,
who sipped her grenadine from crystal. . . .
The children! I should never have left them
weather like this.

3 Scoliosis

Mantell's *Journal*:

Eleven years of spinal disease, misunderstood at the time,
its origin still difficult, but tabulated:

> 1841: Carriage accident. Onset of paralysis
> in lower limbs, attributed by Mantell
> to stooping in 1839 and 1840.
> Pelvic viscera affected. Spasms, numbness.

> 1842: Tumor, fluid-filled, on spine's left side.
> Aorta displaced, giving rise to left-leg edema.
> Lawrence, Liston, Brodie, all looked in.

Of the specimen, Pathologic Curator of the Royal College of
Surgeons Museum, Mr. Proger, noted:

> Apart from the deformity which is accurately described
> above, there is no evidence in the vertebral bodies to account
> for curvature. We eliminate such causes as tuberculosis,
> tumors, Paget's disease, post-traumatic spondylitis, shorten-
> ing of the leg or hip-joint fixation. We attribute this condition
> to postural scoliosis, present the greater part of the scientist's
> life. That the lumbar spine collapsed is clinical mystery.

> 1985: At the Institute mentioned above, the curious may view the
> scientist's spine, tastefully mounted.

4   Letter to Mary Ann

She straightens above her needlework—
under Victorian shrubbery, beasts grazing
a puddle of stars—from her pricked thumb
wipes blood at the canvas corner.
Her caught needle spins point downward
on its thread, jittering north
above the carpet gritty with sand,
the insinuation of his quarry samples
even into her skin, the flint
he pressed himself against as if she were road metal,
he the traveler with somewhere else to go.
I read she eventually left him;
the Queen's century buzzed with her will.
She settles beside the oil lamp with my letter,
torn in transit.

. . . In a small plane above Gloucester,
I rocked on a current of air.
The body is easily deceived,
our pilot told me; some have plunged to earth
certain of altitude in vertiginous fog.
How many petals have fallen from the peonies
to the table as you read this?
Buoyant, the hacked quarries spangling land below,
their motions invisible under water,
I thought of you from the other side of science,
where faith, replaced by instruments, succeeds
to faith, a trickle of pink fuel
in the cylinders. In a dream,
you came to me beside those quarries
to speak of our common life, a reconstruction
of the buried creature you yourself discovered.

In one hand, you offered a road,
from the other, good-byes gyrated like birds,
with their tough hydraulics.
Our pilot checked the engine for their nests.
The road was a concept we buckled into,
like waking alone, or wind sheer,
those hazards of velocity, direction.
You, with your scissors
neatening an afternoon of labor,
might think of me
when you rise and walk into the garden,
looking into a sky given depth
by where we've been. In a petal's fall,
I've waited for the engine to ease us back.
Here, survival still depends
on the pilot's surprising heart.

4 Variable Life

The Late Show

We even had a swing band in our parade,
a fire truck, a jazz band. What a Saturday.
Mickey turns from another customer to me.
Over his shoulder, pennants from local high schools
lift a little as the door behind us tinkles shut.
Mickey, I think, you'll kill yourself with Camels.
Cigarettes, he says. He knows the label.
Flo, distributing bulk down the store's one aisle,
comes in from the back, smiling. I count.
Four cans of tomato soup, shelved.
Last week there were five. I try not to fasten
on black eyes, Flo's right, Mickey's left.
I imagine how they rise,
turn off *The Sands of Iwo Jima* and haggle
about taxes, the leaking ceiling,
why, behind the fire truck, Mickey kissed
the VFW cashier on her spit curl.
A siren wails in each of them cranking up,
poised like two fighter pilots as they bank,
no matter how impossible, eye to eye.
I can see his belly, moonlike on her fat thighs,
and how, in turn, she chooses to make up.
Separate, the two of them billow
into the sleep of Sunday morning.
Girlish, Flo walks up to me,
no make-up pasty enough to cover blue.
I know you, I want to tell her
as we chat about the river down the street,
why less lives in it year by year.
I want her to find the place under my eye
where someone once connected.

After Rape

Admit the whirring inside your shoulders
as if an engine, its blades gathering
for expansion, had pressed some barrier,
all your heavy bones ready for air
that slams home, cold, as you heave your window
open to the snow's questionable blankness.
That is fear, regarding the outside without you,
using your dark eyes.

Remember your first ride in a rowboat?
The waves at Scraggy Neck, rhythmic, slapped the prow
and in the water you saw a black girl,
her hair a billow of braids, her mouth an O.
You sang a duet with her: *oh no,*
oh no, oh no, until the rower broke her
with an oar.

Archimedes in his tub understood displacement.
He had a formula. We don't, dear-to-me.
Whichever way a body moves, the universe
arranges yet again, a violence so deep, so previous,
we cannot see it and survive.
The hurt that rolls across our lives is free
in this world, and we side-step, pulling
one another from its arms back to love,
that terrible, wordless study of adulthood.

Spring, 1982

Sunk to their thighs in snow, my friends
precede me through a fog called Payne's Grey
on the palette. Jonquils, iris, and the hybrid,
tulipe noire, stutter at Nellie's shoulder
as she slips, then turns, miming despair,
around her eyes, the artful lines drawn
in the bath's warm steam, beginning to blur.
Her free hand sweeps for balance,
a dancer's port de bras outlandish
as the trees rattle on our heads
their realist specialty, a condensing wet.
I overheat, dressed for the bite
of wind and sun, not this drizzling
shift of mud at work under March
in Dunbarton. Norman vaults the stone fence
of the graveyard for his teacher,
at rest in academic suit and glasses.
Twice I've risked my knees for a pink stone:
at Escalante, as the river rose, inching the cliff
where fire opals winked in volcanic garbage,
and here, beneath the military eyes
of Lowell's Christ. *Selected Poems*
turn limp in our fingers as we tack, reading aloud,
through the backwash of previous engagements.
We are often late. East of Concord,
wines breathe at a readied table.
In the 18th century, painters toned their landscapes
to gold with yellow varnish.
Oh sweeties, as Nellie would say,
we can stand the breakthrough that begins
in everyone around us.

The Trumpet-Flower Vine

No one looks after it.
Everywhere, gripping the oak's black trunk,
or stuck to the concrete wall of the creamery,
it thrives, rooting into the thinnest excuse
for soil. Withered to a stick,
it responds with its spasmodic draw
to the rain, and starts over.

I want to know why, even as I struggle
to understand those people who, yearly,
return to their muddy flood plains
to mop up. Or why, after the hurricane
has removed the furniture from the front room,
the family chooses a new carpet.
How can they stay?

It may be that lovers leaned
into new milk one night,
leaving a print of their labor,
or that nature is a clock, sometimes irritating,
but useful because it awakens us.
I know, but keep going in dead heat.

My friend claims death and sex
are what keep us. Own us, I think.
Tyrannize. But tonight, the orange bell
of the trumpet flower rang unannounced
and I was there, surprised
as I am now, stepping down into a pane of
moonlight, and it holds.

Managing the Composition

Monet, in lace cuffs, chafes
in the noon heat; his straw hat
pulled over round glasses
touches the pipe clenched
between his teeth. His bushy beard
mirrors the haystack, changing,
changing as he waits for Germaine
to drag the sack of canvases
across the field.
No controlling the unexpected,
he mutters. Blue shadows lengthen,
guttering through the grass.
When sight gives out, he creates a field
in memory, his in the reality rolled,
manageable, under his elbow.
An old man in a wrinkled suit,
later he paces his studio,
stopping before the day's work
to analyze defect.
A scent of wild mint
drifts around the easel.

You and I have never visited
that footbridge across his pond,
or watched the water garden
reflecting willows differently
all day. We have bent together
over a kitchen table as the light
changed, though, slicing vegetables
whose bodies were as beautiful
as nudes against the wood,
and came from your own garden.
A cloud hardened its shadow
across the yard and you turned,

following its pressure
against the landscape.
What I mean to say is,
like old Monet, who waded
in the water, we rearrange
those flowers,
which are our lives.

Joy

In the Vineyard Haven ferry's yellow lunchroom,
I stand pressed against a window, fogged
by the holiday disputes of cardsharps, the vacancy
I've reserved sliding closer,
far from Cambridge, oh analysts' bonanza,
where angst, endured methodically,
forestalls what's worse—that dull ache
you could hurt somebody gladly for—boredom.
I'm dreaming of an egg and toast on a Minton plate
given me by an old lady who explains I slept
soundly in Grandpa's fourposter. I take the deck
as gulls, orange-billed, use the boat's draft
and cantilever close for food passengers raise up.
In a red baseball cap, a kid offers me the end of his lunch.
With his clean features, he could be my child
leaning against rules over the rail. I'm not the one
to call his mother, for suddenly those birds,
stupid when they're still, flock in air
above us, like fireworks winking out
before they're down. No one I know sees us shouting,
or crouched, side by side, above pilings
that crack and bend with our landing surge.
Not for the slight-of-heart, these grinding entries,
force spitting water onto our faces,
what gulls didn't claim dropped, black,
into the fascination.
Deep in the works, the turbines
strain backward.
I've seen the man and woman waving, and so has he,
but first, in our blue slickers,
we walk together
all the way to earth.

Wedding, Mid-September

The moment leans so easily
against its chestnut mate,
I slow to take in
a thunderhead, purple
to its pink crest above them,
and the sky, sifting light
like talcum into the field
as I drive by. An updraft

lifts their manes to flags.
Down the hill
before each sense assembles
its relation to event, I
can't call this scene emotional
release. The mass
of withers braced against the mass
of flank so that a hoof curves
delicate from the fetlock, resting.

To weight the mind and stay
a long while in that pasture,
as a child needs to climb
into the parent bodies,
is so impossible, against knowledge,
pure and intellectual,
that it happens.

Wholly animal, they move
where fire can never reach.
Clouds break against their bodies.
Upwind, small figures cut the hay.
All winter, in the barn's downwind
dark, we can find out spring,
sweet vernal, bluestem.
At the bale's quick, its signature
perfume.

About the Author

Janet Sylvester was educated at Goddard College (B.A., 1975; M.F.A., 1978), the University of Utah, and the State University of New York at Binghamton. In 1980 she received an award from the Academy of American Poets and in 1982 the Grolier poetry prize. She is currently Banister writer-in-residence at Sweet Briar College in Virginia.

About the Book

That Mulberry Wine was composed in Bembo by G&S Typesetters of Austin, Texas. It was printed on 60 lb. Warren's Sebago and bound by Kingsport Press of Kingsport, Tennessee. Dust jackets and covers were printed by New England Book Components of Hingham, Massachusetts. Design by Joyce Kachergis Book Design and Production of Bynum, North Carolina.

Wesleyan University Press, 1985.